Count With Me

CRYSTAL SIKKENS

HOW MUCH?

A Crabtree Roots Book

Crabtree Publishing
crabtreebooks.com

School-to-Home Support for Caregivers and Teachers

This book helps children grow by letting them practice reading. Here are a few guiding questions to help the reader with building his or her comprehension skills. Possible answers appear here in red.

Before Reading:

- What do I think this book is about?
    - *I think this book is about finding out how much something holds.*
    - *I think this book is about containers.*
- What do I want to learn about this topic?
    - *I want to learn what objects hold things.*
    - *I want to learn what holds more and what holds less.*

During Reading:

- I wonder why...
    - *I wonder why we say something is half full.*
    - *I wonder why a bucket holds more than a glass.*
- What have I learned so far?
    - *I have learned how to tell if something is empty, full, or half full.*
    - *I have learned that capacity means how much something can hold.*

After Reading:

- What details did I learn about this topic?
    - *I have learned that if one thing holds more than another, it has a larger capacity.*
    - *I have learned that if one thing holds less than another, it has a smaller capacity.*
- Read the book again and look for the vocabulary words.
    - *I see the word **capacity** on page 4 and the word **empty** on page 7. The other vocabulary words are found on page 14.*

I want to learn how much things can hold.

The amount something can hold is called **capacity**. This girl's glass is **full**.

This boy's glass is **empty**.

This girl's glass is **half full**.

The bucket holds more than the glass. It has a larger capacity.

The yellow cup holds less.

It has a smaller capacity.

Word List

Sight Words

a
about
called
can
has
how
I
is
it
more
than
the
this
to
want

Words to Know

capacity

empty

full

half full

55 Words

I want to learn how much things can hold.

The amount something can hold is called **capacity**. This girl's glass is **full**.

This boy's glass is **empty**.

This girl's glass is **half full**.

The bucket holds more than the glass. It has a larger capacity.

The yellow cup holds less. It has a smaller capacity.

HOW MUCH?

Count With Me

Crabtree Publishing

crabtreebooks.com 800-387-7650

 In Canada: We acknowledge the financial support of the Government of Canada through the Canada Book Fund for our publishing activities.

Hardcover 978-1-0398-7270-7
Paperback 978-1-0398-7328-5
Ebook (pdf) 978-1-0398-7385-8
Epub 978-1-0398-7434-3

Published in Canada
Crabtree Publishing
616 Welland Avenue
St. Catharines, Ontario
L2M 5V6

Published in the United States
Crabtree Publishing
347 Fifth Avenue
Suite 1402-145
New York, NY 10016

Written by: Crystal Sikkens
Designed by: Margaret Salter
Proofreader: Kathy Middleton
Photographs: All other images by Shutterstock.com
Production manager: Candice Campbell

Printed in the U.S.A./CP022026